Raising Responsible Teenagers

By Tom Tozer

Family Tree™

Group®

Loveland, Colorado

Dedication

To Charles and Ruth, my parents.
For their support and encouragement.
With love and thanks.

Raising Responsible Teenagers
Copyright © 1991 by Tom Tozer

First Printing

Credits
Edited by Eugene C. Roehlkepartain
Cover and interior design by Jill Bendykowski
Illustrations by Rick Stromoski

Scripture quotations are from the Good News Bible in Today's English Version. Copyright © 1966, 1971, 1976.

ISBN 1-55945-017-7

Printed in the United States of America

CONTENTS

CHAPTER*SIX*

CHAPTER**ONE**

MOVING TOWARD RESPONSIBILITY

Josh was crazy about Brenda. When he finally got up the courage to ask her to "go steady," she made him wait until Monday for her answer. And when the answer was yes, Josh stayed in a daze the rest of the school day.

After school, Josh had to do some chores on his grandmother's farm. But he was so happy about Brenda's answer that even the chores didn't bother him. In fact, he asked Brenda and some other friends to come along.

Everything seemed perfect in Josh's world.

The farm work went quickly with everyone pitching in. Then the kids all decided to head for the Pizza Palace to celebrate Josh and Brenda's hot, new romance. Brenda wanted to drive. Even though she was only 14, Josh was too happy to say no. Everyone piled in and took off, with Brenda behind the wheel.

Brenda wasn't familiar with the car or with the country dirt roads. She took a corner too fast and skidded, losing control and hitting a ditch. The car rolled twice. After an eerie silence, Josh and his friends regained their senses and surveyed the damage. They were hardly scratched.

But Brenda was dead.

Josh's life changed dramatically. He became a loner. He grew more and more rebellious. He was caught stealing. His grades plunged. His parents grounded him nearly every week for one thing or another.

Finally, they confronted Josh in his bedroom. "Josh, it's time to clean up your act!" his dad said. "You're not the only person in the world who's had some tough breaks!"

Josh's mom joined in. "When are you going to stop acting like the world owes you an apology?"

"Leave me alone!" Josh screamed.

"Look, son," his dad said forcefully, "snap out of it. What happened was tragic, but you're letting this completely ruin your life."

"The sad part is you're doing it to yourself, Josh," his mom added. "You have too much to offer to just throw it all away."

Josh's dad fought back tears as he put his hand on his son's shoulder. "Son, you can choose to be different. You can take control of your life."

That confrontation began turning Josh around. "I finally realized there was nothing I could do to change what happened," he told me later. "Things started getting better. But I'll never forget the choices I could've made to change the way it turned out."

UNGUIDED DECISIONS

O ur homes, churches, schools and communities are filled with Joshes who face tough choices: Should I experiment with drugs? Should I go to college? Should I date Monty? Should I have premarital sex? Will I be an active Christian? Sometimes they make responsible choices. But, as Josh discovered, sometimes their choices lead to tragic results. Why?

In interviewing more than 100 moms and dads, I discovered a significant part of the answer: Virtually no one teaches kids good decision-making skills. Not the schools. Not the church. And not the family. The result is a lot of irresponsible, sometimes tragic, choices.

National research leads to a similar conclusion. A Girl Scouts of the U.S.A. survey found that young people depend primarily on their own instincts in making decisions. When asked to name the most believable authority in matters of truth, 45 percent named their personal experience. Parents' teaching came next at only 20 percent. And 12 percent didn't know who to believe!

Kids haven't gotten much guidance about how to be responsible from us or anyone else. They feel left to their own intuitions and whims. At age 15, Scott wound up in the hospital with a serious ulcer. The doctor told Scott the ulcer developed because he had candy bars and soft drinks every day for lunch. Scott had done this for as long as he could remember. His shocked parents had assumed Scott was spending his lunch money on decent meals. But they'd never talked about what "a decent meal" was!

It's not that we don't care about our kids or don't teach them anything. Indeed, we painstakingly teach our young children to go to the bathroom, dress themselves and brush their teeth. Later, we explain the intricacies of flying a kite and pumping their legs to swing. Then our kids become teenagers, and we teach them how to set up checking accounts, coordinate their clothes and drive cars.

Yet when it comes to being responsible, we expect our kids to learn by trial and error, or simply by reflex—acting instinctively on the spur of the moment. And then we shake our heads in disbelief—and horror—at their dumb, irresponsible decisions!

If we want our kids to become responsible, we must teach them to become responsible. By making wise choices, our teenagers will become more and more responsible.

TOUGH DECISIONS

Sometimes it's tempting to protect kids from their own irresponsibility. We've had more experience. We know better. We can see the consequences and potential problems. Why not just decide for them?

But that approach never works—at least not for long. Someday our kids will have to weave through the mental maze of tough choices without our holding their hands. If we don't teach them the skills to negotiate their own path, they're likely to turn down whatever alley is "in" or easy.

Though it's difficult to admit, no young person—regardless of age, social status or spiritual maturity—is completely immune to our culture's temptations. "Every child in this country between the ages of 12 and 14 will be called upon to make a decision about drugs and alcohol," states an article in U.S. News & World Report. "Parents who do nothing to help kids make that decision, who merely hope for the best, who blithely assume 'not my kid' now and forever, are abandoning their children at the edge of a whirlpool."

To be sure, many decisions aren't as emotionally charged as drug and alcohol use. Nonetheless, other decisions can be just as important and far-reaching.

John has been offered a terrific after-school job. Not only would he have opportunities for advancement, but he'd save money for college.

But John also dreams of being a basketball star. He loves to play, and is exceptionally talented. And he's always wanted to find out just how good he really is.

John has a tough choice to make. While it certainly isn't life-threatening, it could be life-altering. Who knows what opportunities he might gain if he takes the job and saves money? On the other hand, who knows what he might miss by not pursuing his basketball dream?

John's parents have a difficult decision too. They've tried to give John space to think for himself. How much should they try to influence his decision? If they leave it up to him, will they be "abandoning him at the edge of the whirlpool," where he may fall in and spend his life going in circles?

INDEPENDENT DECISIONS

"*B*ut," you say, "I would never abandon my child!" Of course not. As Christian parents, we try always to be there for our kids. We've taught them Christian values. We've tried to be good role models. We want the best for them.

But what happens when our teenagers abandon us? When they scream, "Bug off—it's my life and I'll do what I want"? Will any parent ever again enjoy a full night of restful sleep?

Susan had no intention of telling her parents she no longer went to youth group at church. She had more fun hanging out with friends from school. They used drugs and drank. Though Susan hadn't given in, she was tempted ... and probably would eventually.

She'd lied to the youth leader, explaining she had a job conflict. But, she added, her parents agreed that the job was best.

The youth leader tried to dissuade Susan, explaining how important being around Christians was for helping her grow in faith. But she didn't care. She had too much fun with her friends.

Susan had made a major decision entirely on her own. Without thinking through the consequences, she'd gotten involved in negative friendships that could affect the rest of her life. And she may have taken the first step in moving away from God.

Though we may not always like our kids' decisions, it's natural for teenagers to make more and more decisions on their own as they mature. And each decision they make can bring them closer to adulthood.

This independence is important to teenagers. The American Chicle Youth Poll, a national survey of American teenagers, found that the #1 thing teenagers say would improve home-life would be to be treated more as an adult. And kids have definite opinions of what decisions they should be able to make, as the "When Kids Want to Decide" box on page 12 shows.

"It's me, don't you think?"

WHEN KIDS WANT TO DECIDE

*T*eenagers have definite opinions on when they should be able to make their own decisions about specific issues. According to the American Chicle Youth Poll, their opinions vary a great deal. But, on the average, they believe they should be allowed to make certain decisions at the following ages:

By age 17, teenagers believe they should decide independently ...
- How late to stay out.
- Whether to quit school.
- Whether to have sex.

By age 18, teenagers believe they should decide independently ...
- Whether to drink beer or wine.
- Whether to smoke marijuana.
- Whether to buy pornography.

By age 19, teenagers believe they should decide independently ...
- Whether to drink liquor.
- Whether to get married.

ALL-OR-NOTHING DECISIONS

*M*ost teenagers don't want to be left with total responsibility for all their decisions. At the same time, they also want—and need—more decision-making responsibility as they mature.

So how do we know when to let our kids make decisions? Or when to step in and help? Is it okay to want to be part of all decisions that affect our teenagers? Or should we back away, waiting for them to ask for our advice?

Unfortunately, some parents have an all-or-nothing mentality about helping kids make decisions. Some sit in the driver's seat where they can be in complete control. Others sit in the back seat and close their eyes, hoping their teenager doesn't crash.

● *Total control*—Everyone was shocked when Walt showed up for youth choir practice. No one knew he could sing.

"My dad wants me to sing in the choir," Walt shrugged when pressed.

"Do you want to sing?" the director prodded.

Walt smiled self-consciously. "I dunno. My dad told me I have to."

The choir director took Walt aside and assured him there were other things he could do to help the choir if he didn't want to sing. "We'll need someone to handle the tape recorder and microphones," the director offered.

Walt shook his head. "Nah, my dad's pretty much made up his mind."

Not only had Walt's dad made up his own mind, but he'd also made up his son's mind. If he continues, Walt won't have any mind of his own.

Parents like Walt's dad have an *authoritarian* parenting style that is non-negotiable and inflexible. The parent makes rules and decisions, and doesn't tolerate deviation from those decisions.

While this style can have many negative long-term effects on teenagers, two particular problems arise in terms of nurturing responsibility:

1. It makes teenagers indecisive. Walt will never be able to

make a move on his own without first getting Dad's okay—or the okay of another authority figure. If we make all the decisions for our kids, they'll never develop the skills they need to become responsible adults.

2. It leaves teenagers yearning for approval. If parents govern everything their teenagers do, kids soon begin to do things simply to make parents happy. As a result, teenagers like Walt will always wonder if someone else approves.

● *No control*—Unlike Walt's dad, Gloria's mom desperately wants her daughter to like her. Whatever Gloria wants, Gloria gets. Her mother is afraid that if she says no to Gloria, she'll not only hurt her daughter's feelings, but she may alienate her altogether.

Gloria doesn't have a curfew. She takes her mom's car whenever she wants. She even has her own credit card—in her mother's name. She picks her own clothes, some of which are quite revealing. In essence, Gloria runs the house and her mom.

When the other girls talk about their parents' rules and restrictions, however, Gloria almost feels envious. While her mother is bending over backward to give her daughter freedom, Gloria senses her mom just doesn't care where she goes or what she does.

Gloria's mom wants to be a pal.

Gloria wants a parent.

This kind of non-committal or *permissive* decision-making style has numerous negative effects on teenagers, with two particular effects on their becoming responsible adults:

1. It doesn't give any guidance. Because permissive parents don't set boundaries for their teenagers, the teenagers must discover boundaries on their own. And the only way to do that is to cross the boundaries and suffer the consequences.

Gloria will always have to make trial-and-error decisions. She'll never know any concrete rules for making the best possible decisions. As a result she risks tragic consequences if she crosses life-threatening lines in her search for boundaries.

2. It leaves teenagers susceptible to peer pressure. Gloria is easily swayed by others' opinions. Because her mother never offers guidance, Gloria yearns for someone else to provide direction. Thus, she'll be an easy target for aggressive people who are eager to control other people.

BALANCED DECISIONS

Somewhere between being too authoritative and being too permissive is a comfortable balance. Barb and Joel Crawford have discovered how elusive that balance can be.

At first, they never said no to their daughter Amy. The experts they read argued that saying no too much smothers creativity and stifles individuality. Give your kids freedom, these experts urged, and rebellion won't be a problem.

So Amy made her own decisions—all of them. She lived without boundaries, and got into serious trouble. She got mixed up with a rough crowd, and began experimenting with drugs and alcohol.

Frustrated and confused, Barb and Joel turned to other experts. They learned how Amy felt neglected. Amy's behavior was a plea for attention—her way of asking for disapproval, of begging for boundaries, the experts counseled.

Amy's concerned parents reacted by overreacting. They

WHO DECIDES?

*W*hat decisions does your teenager make alone? What decisions do you make together? And which decisions are yours exclusively as a parent?

In the blank beside each decision that involves your teenager, write the initial of the person who usually makes that decision. If you make the decision together, write all applicable initials. Ask your teenager and spouse (if applicable) to complete the checklist separately. Then ask yourself the questions at the end.

Who decides . . .

1. Which college to attend, if any? ____
2. Which courses to take in high school? ____
3. Which social events to attend? ____
4. What time to be home? ____
5. Which friends to spend time with? ____
6. What clothes to wear? ____
7. Which extra-curricular activities to participate in? ____
8. How to spend personal money? ____
9. Who will use the family car? ____
10. Whether the teenager will go to church, and which church? ____
11. Whether to wear makeup, and how much to wear? ____
12. Which babysitting or other "freelance" jobs to accept? ____
13. What to watch on television and how much to watch each week? ____
14. Which movies to see? ____
15. Whether to smoke? ____
16. What music to buy or listen to on the radio? ____
17. What food to eat? ____

continued

18. How to share telephone use? ____
19. Whether to take a part-time job? ____
20. Whether to buy a car, and what kind to buy? ____
21. When to do homework, and how much time to spend doing it? ____
22. Which chores to do and when? ____
23. When to start dating? ____
24. Whether to drink? ____

● Add the number of times each person's initials appear:
  ● You: ____ times.
  ● Your spouse: ____ times.
  ● Your teenager: ____ times.
  ● Joint decision: ____ times.

● If your or your spouse's initials appear alone more than eight times, are you controlling your teenager too much? Or is that amount of control appropriate for his or her age?

● If your teenager's initials appear alone more than eight times, are you giving your teenager enough guidance? Or is that amount of freedom appropriate for his or her age?

● Then compare your responses to other family members' responses. Discuss together:

1. Do you and your family members differ sharply in some areas? If so, why? What can you do to resolve differences?

2. Which decisions you make as a parent would you like to begin having your teenager make? How can you begin moving in that direction?

3. In which areas does your teenager feel need for more guidance? How can you offer that guidance without usurping responsibility?

didn't give her any responsibility. They made every decision for Amy—and nearly always said no. They tried to control her so completely that, instead, they lost her. Amy moved out in anger to live in an apartment with some friends.

Now, months later, things are better. Amy has come back home, and the family is trying to find a healthy balance between the two extremes. Amy's parents realized they'd consulted every "expert" but one: Amy. They'd never talked together about how to handle responsibilities. Now they do, and they're all gradually entering the comfort zone in their decision-making.

What Barb, Joel and Amy are discovering is a style of shared decision-making that's often considered part of a *democratic* parenting style. It has several important characteristics.

● *The comfort zone is a partnership.* Effective decision-making in the family is a shared responsibility that brings parents and teenagers closer together. Instead of leaving decision-making in one person's hands, it involves everyone in the process. Amy knows that her feelings and wishes are taken seriously, so she feels better about herself and her family.

● *The comfort zone follows Christ's model.* When Jesus taught his disciples and followers, he didn't force them to do everything his way. He didn't rescue them whenever they made bad choices.

When Jesus told the rich man to sell everything and give the money to the poor, the man "went away sad." Jesus didn't run to catch him and try to convince him otherwise; he let the man live with his choice (Mark 10:17-23). Indeed, he let Judas leave the supper in the upper room to betray him (John 13:21-30).

At the same time, Jesus didn't leave his followers stranded without guidance. In the case of the rich man, he didn't lower his standard by saying: "Okay, then maybe you don't have to sell *everything*. What do you want to sell?" He let people know what he expected and let them make their own choices.

● **The comfort zone requires honest communication.**
Only when Barb, Joel and Amy are honest with each other does
shared decision-making work. That honesty assures that everyone's opinions are taken seriously. It also creates a healthy, open
atmosphere at home so kids feel comfortable coming to their
parents for advice and counsel.

● **The comfort zone fosters responsible choices.** As
parents and teenagers work through decisions together, parents
pass along decision-making skills to their teenagers.

Dean Johnson, now a young adult, remembers sitting on the
couch with his mother when he was trying to decide whether to
take an after-school job. "Let's get some paper and chart the pros
and cons of both options," she suggested. They sat together and
brainstormed advantages and disadvantages.

With his mom's input, Dean decided not to take a job until
summer. And he used pros-and-cons charts many times after he
left home, when he faced tough choices such as how to spend
his money or whether to take a new job.

● **The comfort zone keeps roles distinct.** Unlike permissive parenting, the democratic parenting style remembers
that parents are parents and teenagers are teenagers. Parents still
see themselves as responsible for their children's upbringing, and
they're willing to make important decisions after discussing the
possibilities with their teenagers.

● **The comfort zone builds mutual trust and respect.**
As we negotiate and discuss choices with our teenagers, we learn
more about each other. We learn to respect each other's thinking
processes and values. And we discover that we can trust each
other as we learn from each other.

For several years, Hector Archbold had always tried to involve his daughter, Maria, in decisions he made. Sometimes she

followed his advice, and sometimes she didn't. But she knew she could count on him to give a perspective to her choices.

In college, Maria's old car broke down, and she needed to replace it. The decision was hers to make, since she had a job that paid the bills. But she called her dad about her choices. He helped her think through her budget and her realistic needs. As it turned out, she bought a less-expensive but more-reliable car than she originally considered.

"I trust my dad's instincts," she explained. "I don't always agree with him, but I respect his perspective. He changed my mind ... this time!"

SHARPENED SKILLS

I wrote *Raising Responsible Teenagers* to help you find this "comfort zone" in helping your own teenager grow into a responsible adult. We'll explore questions such as:

- Why is it so hard for my teenager to become responsible?
- What happens when my teenager acts irresponsibly?
- How does the Christian faith help guide decisions?

Most of the prescriptions I suggest are based on common sense and are easy to follow. Some may even seem obvious. But you'll discover how many of these obvious ideas and tips we fail to try. Perhaps they're so obvious we forget how important they are. This book will refresh your memory and sharpen your skills.

CHAPTER*TWO*

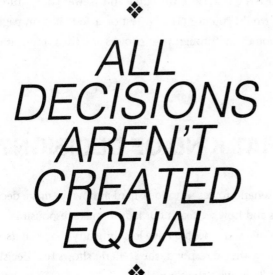

ALL DECISIONS AREN'T CREATED EQUAL

I t's exam time. You've studied for hours. If you ace this course, doors will open for your future. If you don't, those doors will stay shut. Your future salary and job opportunities depend heavily on the test results.

The instructor passes out the exam. You have one hour. You begin. The questions are tricky. And though you've pored over the material, you realize you concentrated in the wrong areas. Your body grows warm, and your hands are clammy. You're in trouble.

After a few minutes, you notice movement across the aisle. You glance over and discover classmates passing a crib sheet back and forth. They're already on the second page, and you're sweating over the second question! The instructor is reading a newspaper, totally oblivious to what's happening. You seem to be the only one who sees the cheating.

Then it hits you: This instructor grades on a curve! Those jerks will ace the test, skew the curve and skewer your future!

What would you do? (The "A Test on a Test" box on page 24 will help you think through your choices and their implications.)

WHAT KIND OF DECISION?

*T*his scenario forces us to look hard at how we make decisions and how we teach our kids to make responsible choices. While some people have less difficulty than others knowing how they'd respond, the scenario shows that decision-making isn't always a simple matter.

The cheating scenario also raises questions about how we make decisions. Are all decisions a matter of black and white? Or do they come in all shades between? And if they do, how do we teach our kids to make good decisions and stick with their Christian values too?

Decisions vary in complexity and fuzziness. Some decisions are morally perplexing or life-changing, such as knowing whether to accept a new job. Others are no more profound than deciding what to have for dinner. And each type of decision requires a different approach. Let's look at four general kinds of decisions our kids face nearly every day.

● *Cut-and-dried decisions*—These decisions don't require a lot of thought. Before you take a hot dish out of the oven, you decide to use a hot pad. Pretty elementary, but it still involves making a decision.

Yet some seemingly cut-and-dried decisions become more muddled in our kids' minds because of peer pressure and wanting to be liked. For example, taking drugs just isn't an option for most of our kids. We hope and pray their decision would be a cut-and-dried refusal. But we know the power of peer pressure to confuse a seemingly obvious choice.

What's our role, as parents, in these kinds of decisions? We need to set good examples for our kids. In the case of drugs, our teenagers may be tempted to experiment because of peer pressure. Through what we say and do, we can model a personal stand against drug use that will keep our kids from letting the decision become muddled for them. That stand could be getting involved in groups that fight drug abuse. Or it could be a personal decision to refuse to abuse drugs or alcohol of any kind.

● *Open-ended decisions*—Some decisions are fuzzy, and don't involve clear-cut right or wrong choices. Each option can have positive and negative consequences. And each takes time and thought.

In our teenagers' world, such matters as selecting a college, going steady or going out for football can be open-ended decisions. Kids need to think about a lot of things before deciding, including dozens of possible consequences.

Decisions that are open-ended for some people may be cut-and-dried for others because of particular circumstances or perspectives. For example, deciding whether to get a pet cat is probably an open-ended decision for most people. But it's cut-and-dried for someone who's allergic to cats!

As parents, we can help our kids think through their open-ended choices. Though it's useful, setting an example isn't

A TEST ON A TEST

*U*se the following questions to help you think through the issues addressed in the cheating scenario on page 21.

1. What would you do about your discovery of the cheating?
    (a) Keep quiet.
    (b) Tell the instructor after class.
    (c) Tell the instructor immediately.
    (d) Join the cheating ring.
    (e) Other: _____

2. What are the possible consequences of each option?
    (a)

    (b)

    (c)

    (d)

    (e)

3. In this scenario, which decision would be ...
    (a) a good decision?
    (b) the best decision?
    (c) the right decision?

4. If you chose different answers for a, b and c in question 3, what distinctions did you make? If all your answers were the same, why?

continued

5. Which of the following issues is most important in your choice?
   (a) Following advice from an authority figure
   (b) Doing what's best for everyone
   (c) Doing what will help you get ahead
   (d) Following your conscience
   (e) Doing what you believe God says
   (f) Doing what makes you happy
   (g) A combination of the above
   (h) Don't know

6. What role does your faith play in your decision?
   (a) It completely guides it.
   (b) It helps a little.
   (c) It makes no difference.

7. How would your decision be affected if the exam weren't graded on a curve?
   (a) Not at all
   (b) Make it easier
   (c) Totally change it

8. Read Matthew 18:15-17 and Luke 16:1-13. If your teenager were the person who saw the cheating, what would you hope he or she would do?

9. Look back at all your answers. What trends do you see? How would you explain them? Discuss your responses with your spouse (if applicable) and your teenager.

enough, in itself. We need to help our kids examine the options and weigh the consequences. The rest of this book suggests ways to help kids think about decisions and make responsible choices.

● *Long-range decisions*—These decisions are nearly always open-ended, and they usually require lots of time and scrutiny. Decisions on world concerns, for instance, can take years. Government officials still can't decide how best to preserve our natural resources. Long-range decisions are agonizingly slow to make, and many are never fully resolved.

A career can be a long-range decision for a teenager, if he or she consciously sets a course that includes several phases of study and experience. Finding the right mate and developing one's spiritual life are also long-range decisions.

While teenagers may not yet be very concerned about these long-range decisions, their attitudes and lifestyles during adolescence prepare them to make such decisions. As parents, we can help them think through the more immediate choices that affect their futures.

● *On-the-spot decisions*—On-the-spot decisions are made without the luxury of time and planning. An on-the-spot decision that's also open-ended is the most difficult of all.

The cheating scenario at the beginning of the chapter illustrates the difficulty. The person who sees the cheating has to make a fast and critical decision. No one can help. And there's very little time. Yet, there are several options with both immediate and far-reaching consequences.

Peer pressure bombards our teenagers with tough, on-the-spot, open-ended decisions. A 10th-grader puts it this way: "When we go out, we're not thinking of things to do that our parents won't like. We're not planning to make mistakes on purpose. We're just planning to have fun."

The tremendous weight of peer pressure can break down kids' resistance—in spite of a Christian background and upbringing. Our teenagers face these decisions daily:

● "Come on, take just one drink!" Even a model teenager might succumb to that temptation. It's just one drink, and everybody's doing it.

● "If you get pregnant, I'll marry you. I promise!" When the emotional thermometer skyrockets out of control, a sensible decision is a contradiction in terms.

● "Go faster, faster, faster!" With the press of a pedal, an otherwise level-headed teenager can have more power and attention than he or she ever dreamed of having. Unfortunately, the attention is often in the form of traffic statistics and obituaries.

What can we parents do to help our kids survive these pressure-induced, on-the-spot decisions? We can make our kids feel important at home. We can listen to them and respect their opinions. We can maintain high standards and expectations. We can give them our love and attention so they won't need to seek those things elsewhere. And we can ask God to give them the strength they'll need when they're on their own.

WHAT'S THE BEST DECISION?

We've discussed various types of decisions. However, there is still another facet of decision-making. I call it the *quality* of decisions.

YOUR DECISION-MAKING WIZARDRY

*W*hat kinds of decisions are involved in the following situations? In the "parent" column, list the letters that indicate the types of decisions:

(a) Cut-and-dried decision (c) Long-range decision
(b) Open-ended decision (d) On-the-spot decision

Ask your teenager to score the situations using the "teenager" column. See how your answers compare. By the way, some decisions may have more than one answer.

Decision	Parent	Teenager
1. Your teenager, a high school senior, needs to decide which college to attend.	_____	_____
2. You work in a grocery store. A homeless man asks for free food to feed his children.	_____	_____
3. John is popular, and your daughter has a crush on him. One day he shows up unexpectedly and wants to take your daughter for a spin in his new car. You've heard stories about his fast driving.	_____	_____
4. Your teenager is out with friends. Someone suggests pulling a prank.	_____	_____
5. You're thinking about changing churches, leaving a church you've belonged to for 10 years.	_____	_____

continued

6. The parent-teacher organization at the local high school wants to eradicate drug use in your school and community. The president asks you to lead the effort.   _____   _____

7. You see someone shoplifting during the Christmas rush. The person looks old and poor.   _____   _____

8. The family is deciding where to go on vacation.   _____   _____

9. Someone comes to your door and asks you to sign a petition.   _____   _____

10. Your family is considering buying a dog.   _____   _____

11. A cashier gives you too much change.   _____   _____

12. You're late to church, and the only way to get there on time is to break the speed limit.   _____   _____

Some of the answers to these questions may be obvious for you, but many depend upon the specific circumstances. Discuss with your teenager:

● What do the similarities in our lists tell us? the differences?

● What circumstances might change your decision on some questions?

● Which statements were most difficult to classify? Why?

HOW KIDS DECIDE WHAT'S RIGHT

*I*n making choices, people rely on different information. Some might decide based on their feelings at the moment. Others carefully weigh the options. The Girl Scouts of the U.S.A. surveyed young people to discover how kids would make a decision about right or wrong if they didn't know what to do. Kids said they . . .

- Would do what's best for everyone—23%
- Would follow the advice of an authority—21%
- Would do what makes them happy—18%
- Would do what God says—16%
- Would do what would improve their situation or get them ahead—10%
- Don't know what they'd do—9%
- Would follow their conscience—3%

Decisions are elusive. What you decide may not be what I'd decide.

So who's made a *good* decision? Maybe both of us. It depends on many factors and considerations. Maybe a choice seems good now, but will turn sour later on.

Who made the *best* decision? Certainly I have, otherwise I wouldn't have made it! But you probably feel the same way. Yet how do either of us know it's the best decision when we're not sure we knew all the options or considered all the possible consequences.

And who's made the *right* decision? Gadzooks! Right to whom? For whom? Hmmm.

WHAT'S A CHRISTIAN DECISION?

A spry grandfather changed my perspective on my good-best-right dilemma. "If we always strive to make a Christlike decision," he explained, "then that decision will be the good, the best and the right one."

Suddenly I felt the cobwebs clearing from my mind. I'd been caught in an awkward good-best-right dilemma. This veteran of life changed my perspective. The only success you and I really need to be concerned about, he suggested, is to successfully live out our faith. Ultimately we're accountable only to God for our actions and decisions.

Perhaps no one else could've shared that insight with more conviction than someone who could look back on a lifetime of good and bad choices. I was making it so complex. He made it so simple and convincing.

A good decision is a Christian decision. The best decision is the Christian decision. The right decision is most certainly the Christian decision. Suddenly, it's all so simple.

And so tough.

Jesus never said making Christian decisions would be easy. "If anyone wants to come with me, he must forget himself, carry his cross, and follow me," he challenged. "For whoever wants to save his own life will lose it; but whoever loses his life for my sake will find it. Will a person gain anything if he wins the whole world but loses his life?" (Matthew 16:24-26).

Jesus never minced words.

Alex decided his new job was worth the sacrifices. After all, he was making twice the money as he did at his previous job—

money he'd use to buy a car and get his own apartment after high school.

It was a good job all right, but he had to work evenings and weekends. He had to stop going to church, and he couldn't fit the youth group into his schedule. In fact, Alex had little time left for anything or anybody.

But it was good money, he kept reminding himself.

After a few months, he'd become a stranger to his family, friends and church. He cared about no one, and it was increasingly obvious that no one seemed to care about him. He was doing what he thought he wanted to do, but he'd lost the relationships he valued the most.

Alex decided he didn't have to lose the most important parts of his life. He quit his job and began rebuilding his relationships and refocusing his faith priorities. "The money wasn't worth what I was losing," Alex later explained. "Other things are more important than owning a car or moving into an apartment. And the more important things are free!"

I like what Jesus told a teacher of the law who said he was ready to follow him (Matthew 8:18-22). The teacher declared, "Teacher, I am ready to go with you wherever you go."

Jesus replied, "Foxes have holes, and birds have nests, but the Son of Man has no place to lie down and rest." Jesus seems to be asking, "Do you really know what you're asking for?" It's not going to be easy.

WHY ARE CHRISTIAN DECISIONS SO HARD?

*N*ow that we know the goal, why can't we just hand our kids a Bible and tell them to make Christian decisions? Why must we weigh the options and consequences before making the only decision we should want to make—the good-best-right one?

The problem comes in deciding which decision is a Christian decision. There are several reasons that make some Christian decisions difficult:

● *Christian decisions aren't necessarily popular.* Doing what Christ would do won't give our teenagers status. It won't bring fame. It fact, it'll probably label them oddballs.

The girls were whispering about Judy's body odor in the girls' locker room at school. Amid giggles, they decided to write "Judy stinks" in lipstick on the mirror. But before Judy saw the mirror, Peggy wiped it off. "It would hurt Judy's feelings," she explained.

"What about how much Judy hurts our noses!" someone yelled. The others laughed.

"I'll tell Judy about her problem," Peggy volunteered.

The others sneered and told her to run for "Miss Righteous USA."

Despite the badgering, Peggy didn't back down. She talked with Judy and helped her avoid embarrassment. As a Christian, Peggy had learned to treat others the way she hoped she'd be treated. But it wasn't easy to sacrifice popularity.

● *Christian decisions can be uncomfortable.* Lee Townsend and some school friends wanted to do something to help people. They decided to volunteer part of their lunch and study periods to deliver meals to shut-ins for the local Meals on Wheels program. They got the principal's permission.

Ken and Nancy Townsend weren't thrilled about their son's decision. First, he had to drop swing band because the group practiced every other day during lunch. They'd spent a lot of money for his music lessons. Neither were they pleased that Lee was giving up a study period.

"There will always be time to deliver food to old people," Ken told his son. "Look what you're giving up!"

"Dad, I don't see that I'm giving up anything. I'm gaining something," Lee replied. "I feel good about this."

"Where did our kid learn to be some kind of saint?" Ken later said to Nancy in a half-mocking tone.

"It's a phase," Nancy suggested. "Kids go through them."

Sometimes their faith calls kids to break out of molds to follow God. As parents, we may not be comfortable with those choices. Yet we have to trust God to guide them.

● *Christian decisions aren't always cut-and-dried.* It's not always clear what is and isn't the Christian thing to do. The Bible doesn't specifically cover all the dilemmas of modern life. And while we can apply its basic precepts to our lives, it doesn't give us clear-cut guidance on some of the most troublesome issues we face.

Remember the cheating scenario at the beginning of the chapter? What would Jesus have done in that situation? I asked kids, parents and grandparents that question, and none of the groups could come to a consensus among themselves. Here are some typical responses:

● Jesus would blow the whistle by confronting the cheaters and asking them tough questions—like when he responded to

DECISION-MAKING PARABLES

Some of the finest biblical sources of decision-making wisdom are Jesus' parables. Though some may not relate directly to parent-teenager decisions, the underlying truths apply to nearly every modern-day decision.

Use the following parables (and others) to discuss decision-making principles with your teenager. I've noted key decisions I see in the passages.

● The Parable of the Rich Fool (Luke 12:16-21)—Should we live selfishly or unselfishly? What does it mean to choose between worldly treasures and a life rich in faith?

● The Parable of the Lost Son (Luke 15:11-32)—Should the father let the son leave with the inheritance? And should the father accept the son home when he returns penniless?

● The Parable of the Shrewd Manager (Luke 16:1-13)—Which master do we follow? How do we use God's gift of intelligence? What priorities do we live by as Christians?

● The Parable of the Pharisee and the Tax Collector (Luke 18:9-14)—Will we choose humility or greatness? What priorities do we live by?

the Pharisees and teachers of the law in Matthew 23:1-28.

● Jesus would confront the cheaters outside the class. By showing them their error, he'd persuade them to confess their wrongdoing.

● Jesus might have had a little fun with the cheaters by "zapping" their crib sheet with the wrong answers.

● Jesus would let the cheaters stew in their own juices. He would do nothing himself. He would simply let the offenders do themselves in, which would happen sooner or later.

Sometimes we wish our faith could give us quick-and-easy answers to the complex dilemmas we face. But it doesn't. So we must discover ways to incorporate our faith into our choices, relying on God's grace and love to guide us and to forgive us when we make mistakes.

WHAT WOULD GOD THINK?

While working through tough decisions, our teenagers need stability and focus. Their faith can be a solid rock to stand on amid the whirlpool of confusing choices.

One parent says she has no idea how many crucial decisions her son makes without her or her husband's knowledge or consent. "How can any of us really know what decisions we're excluded from in our kids' lives?" she asked rhetorically. "I just hope my child will always ask, 'What will God think of my decision?' "

That's not a bad place to start.

CHAPTER**THREE**

❖

TUNING UP YOUR ATTITUDE

❖

Ellen wanted to shop around for a new church. She didn't care for the pastor's sermons, and the youth group didn't do anything anymore. She felt like she wasn't growing in her faith.

But Ellen's parents wouldn't even listen to her.

"We've gone to this church for 11 years," her mother snapped.

"You were baptized here," Ellen's dad added. "Do you want to make us look bad in front of everyone?"

Ellen tried to remain calm. "But it's a different pastor now. And most of the kids I know have left," she explained. "I'm not quitting church; I just want to find something better—something that fits me."

"Your home church is just fine. And that's final!" her dad fired back.

Her mother put her hand on Ellen's shoulder. "Honey, you seem more interested in finding a church that offers games and parties. Church isn't supposed to be fun, dear."

Though well-intentioned, Ellen's parents are making a serious mistake. By refusing to listen to and discuss the issue with their daughter, they're not only missing a chance to help her work through an important decision, but they—and the church—may lose Ellen. It's time for Ellen's parents to develop a new outlook that will best help Ellen learn to make important choices about her faith and life.

Like Ellen's parents, we all need to tune up our own attitudes, actions and priorities before we can effectively help our kids learn responsibility.

LISTEN AND TALK OPENLY

*C*ontrast the attitude of Ellen's parents with the attitude of one mother I talked to. Her family talks about anything and everything. "No subject is too controversial," she explained. "And no feelings are spared. We grant amnesty to everyone during our discussions, so you can let it all hang out. It isn't always easy, but it's honest."

She knows what she means when she says it isn't always easy. One particularly difficult time was when her daughter explained she was no longer a virgin.

"I didn't say anything for 10 minutes," the mother relates. "I just stared at her. But even then—after the initial shock—we were able to talk about it. She told me how used and cheap she'd felt afterward and how the guy didn't care. He just wanted to do it again."

Since that startling revelation, mother and daughter talk more about sex than they ever had before. "We talk about Christian values and birth control and about what guys my age are really interested in," the daughter added. "My mom told me to use my head instead of my hormones when I go out. I wish we'd talked more before."

As difficult as it may be, such openness is vital to helping our kids learn responsibility. Only in an open, non-judgmental atmosphere will teenagers share their struggles and temptations.

When asked how they'd respond if their son told them he'd had intercourse with his girlfriend, one couple gave a surprisingly calm and rational answer: "We'd be angry and hurt beyond words that he'd do such a thing. We'd also have to hide our delight that he felt he could tell us. And we'd try to help him see why we believe he made a poor decision."

Creating this kind of open atmosphere can't happen instantly. It takes time to build trust and honesty. But if you have trouble with openness in your family, here are some specific ways to help get the process started:

● *Share your mistakes with your kids.* One father makes an interesting observation: "We can admit our own failures to our kids—as long as those failures are history. Do we have the courage to let our kids see us as human beings who fail every day?"

As parents, we sometimes think we can have an open relationship with our kids and still not talk about our own mistakes. But kids won't open up if we don't open up. We need to tell our kids about our own bad decisions and mistakes. If we don't, we'll always deal with our kids on a superficial level.

Some parents believe opening up to our kids weakens paren-

"Maybe we shouldn't have told him to tell us everything."

tal authority and respect. But the same argument could've been made to say God shouldn't have sent Jesus into the world. Philippians 2:6-7 explains how Jesus had God's nature, but "gave up all he had, and took the nature of a servant. He became like man and appeared in human likeness." This incarnation of God in human flesh may have appeared to "lower" our image of God, but, in reality, it made God's greatness and love even more real.

Admitting our mistakes to our kids also gives us a chance to help them learn from our mistakes. As we discuss what happened and what we learned, they can discover principles and examples that'll help them avoid similar mistakes.

● *Never shut off discussion.* At the beginning of this chapter, we saw how Ellen's parents missed a valuable teachable moment by cutting off discussion about going to church. The chances of Ellen ever bringing her faith questions to her parents are slim.

Whenever we shut off discussion, we tell our kids the subject and their opinions aren't important. So in the future, they'll be less likely to open up because they won't feel respected. Also, kids are likely to continue stewing about a problem if we don't let them air their opinions and talk through options.

● *Don't use information against your kids.* One day, when Paul and his mom were driving home from the mall, Paul brought up some questions he was having about God and Christianity. A friend at school had been pushing him to answer tough questions about God, and Paul thought his friend had some good points. Paul explained his doubts and questions to his mom, and the discussion helped him clarify his thoughts.

Several weeks later, Paul wanted to skip church. He'd spent all day Saturday at work, then stayed up 'til midnight finishing a term paper. His mom was upset and worried. Finally, after much discussion, she said: "Paul, you have to go to church. You're already showing signs of losing your faith. You did say you weren't sure the Resurrection was real."

After that, Paul was careful not to say too much to his mom about his thoughts and questions. He knew anything he said could come back to haunt him later.

In the process of sorting out options, values and opinions, kids say and think things they may not actually believe. The talking helps them figure out their own perspective. They need to know they can say anything without their words being used against them.

● *Maintain accountability.* Make sure your teenagers understand that an open climate doesn't do away with accountability for an irresponsible decision. Openness guarantees all options will be heard, regardless of how unpopular they may be. But it doesn't give blanket approval to whatever choices our kids actually make.

BE A GOOD DECISION-MAKING MODEL

Not long ago, the school superintendent in a small community was arrested in another city by an undercover police officer. The superintendent, a respected professional and citizen, was charged with "misdemeanor sexual battery." Later he was found guilty.

By some standards, it was a relatively minor offense. But here was a high-ranking school official involved in sexual misconduct late at night in a large city. The news caused a statewide furor.

The superintendent resigned immediately and publicly apologized for his actions. His only wish was to move out of the area and start a new life with his wife and family. The town also wanted to put the whole ordeal in the past.

But some prominent community leaders decided they wanted the superintendent to stay on the job. They published a letter in the newspaper asking citizens to support his reinstatement.

"We all make mistakes," one minister argued.

"We all have skeletons in our closets," someone else added.

We need to forgive him, many felt. He's a good administrator and that's what counts—not how he conducts his personal life. Do we let this fine administrator go just because of a "slight transgression"?

Yes! many parents responded emphatically. Let's forgive him and acknowledge the good he's done for the school system. But let's not pretend the misconduct never happened. What kind of message do we send to our kids if we let this man keep his position of authority and respect?

The reinstatement attempt failed. The issue was not an unwillingness to forgive or a desire to pass judgment. Rather, it was a matter of facing the consequences of a bad decision.

How can we hold our kids accountable for their actions if we don't hold ourselves and our peers accountable? How can we be trustworthy if we make poor choices? And how can we hope to teach our kids responsibility if we aren't responsible in our own choices?

Whatever measuring stick we use in determining the height

of our own decision-making standards will almost certainly be the same measuring stick our teenagers use. With that in mind, consider the following questions:

● When Joe calls in sick to his boss and then plays golf, how does his teenage son decide whether to go four-wheeling with his friends instead of cracking the books at school?

● When Leslie watches her parents take pills and drink alcohol to ease their worries, what model does she have to help her choose to resist drug abuse at school?

● When Clark hears his dad brag about all his fabricated deductions on his income tax "because Uncle Sam deserves to be ripped off," how does Clark make a responsible choice when he has a chance to cheat on a test?

As parents, we need first to fine-tune our own sense of responsibility. Then when we make decisions, we need to help our kids understand our thinking processes. And when we make mistakes, our kids need to know we'll seek forgiveness and work to change—just as we expect them to.

HOLD ON AND LET GO

Jamie, 14, was starting to get calls from guys. They'd ask her to a party or just out for a walk.

Jamie's mom started getting worried. She gave her daughter more and more chores to do around the house. After school, Jamie had to clean her bedroom. On weekends, her mom made her stay close to home in case her mom's boss wanted her to work. But Jamie knew her mom never worked weekends.

Soon Jamie felt like Cinderella. She wasn't allowed to take phone calls or answer the door. She felt more and more isolated from her friends. She didn't understand what was going on.

When her mom refused to let her go to a school dance, Jamie tearfully confronted her: "Why are you doing this, Mom? You don't let me do anything anymore."

"Because you're not old enough to take care of yourself," her mother shot back. "There'll be lots of time for dances and parties and guys later—don't rush them!"

"Mom, it's only a dance. Everyone's going."

"Not everyone," her mom returned harshly. Then her tone softened. "Honey, I love you. I just don't want anything to happen to you."

After seeking counseling, Jamie's mother began to realize she had to loosen her grip on her daughter or Jamie would pull away. In time, she learned to let Jamie go out.

The result was that Jamie opened up and included her mom in her social life. She told her mom about the parties and dances and the guys who flirted with her. And the mother and daughter developed a relationship of mutual respect and trust.

We parents try like crazy to hold on to our children. And for good reason. After all, we've spent a lot of years watching them learn, grow and become individuals. They're part of us. And it's hard to give up part of ourselves. But let them go we must. Otherwise, our kids will never get a chance to shape their own identities.

"Letting go" isn't the same as "kicking out." Letting go involves holding on out of love and concern while also letting go out of love and concern. It's the kind of love Christ showed by his willingness to die for us and to let us make our own choices. And it's the kind of love described in the parable of the lost son (Luke 15:11-32).

Andy's parents learned to let go. When he left for college, he was ready. They had taught him the skills he needed, and the whole family had looked forward to the new stage of life.

Oh, tears were shed. But the tears said "We know you have to go, but we'll miss you."

For the first few weeks, Andy and his parents talked regularly on the phone. When he was frustrated and wanted to quit, they encouraged him to "hang in there." Slowly he became an independent and responsible college student. But he still knew he could call home when he needed to hear "I love you."

As important as it is, letting go may be the hardest task you do as a parent. But there are several things you can do to make it easier:

● *Deal with your own wounds.* Jamie's mother developed a stronger prayer life during those difficult times when Jamie started dating. During her quiet moments, she was forced to reach back into her own past and face some harsh realities.

Her own parents had let her come and go as she pleased. She got pregnant when she was barely out of junior high. She'd planned to have the baby but had a miscarriage. After that, she had a reputation of being fast and easy, and the guys pursued her for only one thing.

When she did marry, it was for the wrong reasons. After Jamie was born, her husband left her. Jamie was all she had in the world, and she was determined never to lose her.

Through prayer and counseling, Jamie's mom realized she was making Jamie pay for the bad decisions she'd made as a teenager. But Jamie was different, she learned. Jamie wouldn't necessarily make the same mistakes. And once she and her daughter understood each other, she could help her daughter make responsible choices.

Each of us has had experiences that hurt. It's only natural to want to keep those things from happening to our kids. But we often overreact and create different problems for our kids. By recognizing this danger of overreacting, we can overcome the problem. Or if the problem is serious, we can seek counseling so our kids won't suffer because of our past.

● *Accept differences in your relationship.* Randy and his dad argued about what Randy would do with his life. Was Randy going to get a job and save money for college? Or was he going to fritter away his life playing with that noisy rock band?

"Why don't you move into the garage?" his dad asked angrily one day. "You can play your noise all you want, and I won't have to step over you every time I walk into the house!"

Randy was ready to do just that when his mother pleaded with them to discuss the issue calmly. They finally agreed.

As they talked, Randy and his dad found out a few things about each other. Randy loved his music. Someday he hoped to study music in college. His dad confirmed that he hated Randy's kind of music. But he felt better knowing Randy planned to pursue music seriously.

"But how do you expect to pay for college?" his dad asked. "You still need to get a job."

Randy grew excited. "Dad, the band has a gig this Saturday— a good-paying job. If the place likes us, we'll get to play every weekend for as long as people come. And that means more exposure—more jobs!" Randy looked directly at his dad. "I can earn money for college playing my music!"

Randy never got a "real job," as his dad called it. And his dad never learned to like Randy's music. But they both decided to accept the other's viewpoint and live in peace. After all, they both won with this solution.

When two people differ, we tend to think one must be "wrong." Not so. We don't always have to draw battle lines with our kids. Instead, we need to hold summit meetings and see things from one another's perspective. No one needs to be "wrong."

When you find yourself ready to do battle, remember that you and your teenager both may be right. Then start the peace talks. You'll be amazed at how friendly the conversation can be when neither of you has to be "wrong."

● *Look for common ground.* If you watch MTV or listen to your teenager's music, you already know this: Your language, perceptions and experiences are very different from your teenager's.

It's important to know those differences and to try to understand our kids' world. (For ideas on getting acquainted with your teenager's world, see the "Windows Into Youth Culture" box on page 50.) But it's also important to recognize the similarities between your desires and your teenager's desires.

In our letting-go process, all of us want good things to happen for all of us. We need to talk with one another about those good things. Ask yourself and your teenager the following questions. You may discover great similarities in your responses!

● What do you want ultimately? What do I want?
● How do we plan to get there?
● Here's what I'm willing to do. What are you willing to do?
● Here's where I think I need to let go a little. Where do you think I need to let go a little?

● *Decide what to hold on to and what to let go.* Taking too much baggage can ruin a trip. Holding on to too much baggage in a relationship can destroy it. Letting go ought to be a gradual process. This way, you and your teenager will adjust to the changing relationship.

Begin giving your teenager responsibility for simple decisions, then gradually allow your teenager to handle more important ones. If you haven't already, start with basic decisions such as:

- What to wear to school
- What time to get up on a school day
- What school clubs to join, if any
- When to do specific chores around the house
- When your teenager wants help with homework
- How to manage, spend and save money
- How to decorate and arrange his or her bedroom

At first, it'll be tough not to worry about your teenager's choices. You'll be tempted to interfere if your teenager isn't doing something the way you'd do it. But as your teenager becomes more responsible, you'll become more confident in his or her decision-making ability.

- ***Remember, everyone learns from mistakes.*** I was pretty independent in high school. One Saturday night my date and I decided to drive out into the country and investigate a notorious haunted house. It was already too late to go so far out of town, but that was half the fun.

About 20 miles out, I realized we'd missed a landmark and our turn. I stopped the car and began to back onto a dirt road to turn around. It was dark, and there was no other traffic in sight. I misjudged where the road was and backed into a steep culvert. There I was, stunned and feeling stupid, sitting in a car that must have looked like it was poised on a launch pad.

The car wouldn't budge. I told my shook-up companion to lock the car doors and stay inside. I started walking down this

WINDOWS INTO YOUTH CULTURE

*D*o you feel like your teenager's world is an alien land? Try looking through these windows to get a better picture of your teenager's world and thus understand your teenager better:

● *Watch music television.* If you want to pick up on the latest fashions, hairstyles, rock lyrics and fads, watch MTV occasionally. You probably won't agree with what you see, but if your teenager is into MTV, you need to know what he or she is watching. Then you'll be able to intelligently discuss the values it portrays.

Some friends of mine watch MTV as though they were alien invaders gathering impressions of our society based on the music, lyrics and gyrations. They say aliens would probably change their minds about invading!

● *Go to music and video shops.* What MTV doesn't have, you'll find at music and video shops. Simply ask the clerk what's selling, and ask for a preview.

● *Pick up popular magazines.* Find out what magazines your teenager and his or her peers read. Then scan them yourself to get a cross-section of ideas, images and language kids are exposed to. Some of them may be offensive to you, but knowing what's in them is important for your understanding.

● *Volunteer as a chaperone.* Go on a church youth group or school trip. Or help with an after-game dance. Watch, listen and learn.

continued

● **Talk to your church's youth minister.** Youth workers spend a lot of time talking with teenagers and usually have a sense of what's in and what's out.

● **Visit schools.** Ask teachers what kids talk, write and worry about. Find out why kids wind up in the principal's office. And keep your eyes and ears open in the hallways. There's probably not much you won't see and hear.

● **See a popular movie—with or without your teenager.** Watch the movie the first time. Then go back again and watch the kids watch the movie. What and who gets them excited? Why?

deserted highway looking for a light in a window. Soon I found some friendly folks and called my parents. My dad sounded sleepy. I felt sick.

Half an hour later, my parents came and towed us out. There were no angry words, no homicidal looks. After they determined we were okay, we all drove back home. Was I imagining it or did they seem amused at my predicament?

That night, I learned how much my parents cared for me. They came as fast as they could and got me out of a humiliating jam. There were no lectures then or later. Maybe they knew how humiliated I already felt. Maybe nothing more needed to be said.

Letting go. It may be the hardest, most necessary thing a parent has to do. Yet, if we hope to be effective teachers of responsible decision-making, we'll have to give our kids space to make choices.

CHAPTER**FOUR**

❖

STEP-BY-STEP DECISION-MAKING

❖

We already know that no one teaches decision-making skills. Schools don't. The church doesn't. We parents rely a great deal on the values we instill in our kids early to guide them. But what do we do beyond that to help them become responsible? How many of us have made a conscious effort to teach decision-making to our children?

This chapter presents a simple, step-by-step decision-making process you can teach your teenager. The process might not make the decisions any easier, since some decisions are, by nature, hard. But following the process helps your teenager sort through the options and choices to make a responsible decision.

EXPLORE OPTIONS AND CONSEQUENCES

*J*uan was trapped in what seemed an impossible dilemma. Several football players and other kids planned to raid their cross-town rival and "redecorate" the statue of their school mascot in front of the high school. Juan, a popular student and football player, was expected to go along. But he wasn't sure.

"I'm worried the prank could lead to vandalism," Juan explained to his dad. "Some kids were joking about bringing spray paint, hammers and chisels. I don't want to let the guys down, but I don't want to mess anything up—including my chance at a scholarship."

"So what are your options?" his dad asked.

Juan thought hard, and his choices seemed clear. "I can either join them, or not join them and mind my own business."

"What *is* your business?" his dad probed. "Your responsibility?"

Juan hesitated. "To stay out of trouble and get a scholarship, I guess."

His dad thought for a moment. "Will you stay out of trouble if you don't go with them?"

"Sure," Juan returned. "Of course, the guys'll make fun of me for not going. But at least I won't be involved in destroying property."

"Are you sure?" his dad asked.

Juan looked puzzled. "Yeah, if I don't go ... "

"What if they vandalize the statue and get away with it? No one will know who did it. So how will they know Juan Martinez wasn't involved? Everyone will know the football team had

"Hey! I should get a catalog from this place
too—Hawaii State. What if it has a
better business school?"

something to do with it. You'll be accused whether or not you go."

Juan's jaw dropped. "Then I'm dead! Either way, I look like a jerk!"

"Wait a minute," his dad said. "It seems to me you have several options open to you. The kids respect you. So why not tell your teammates why you think this raid is a bad idea?"

"They'll laugh in my face."

"Maybe," his dad agreed. "Maybe you and some teammates could go along on the raid and make sure no one damages anything. Sort of like crowd control."

Juan nodded slightly.

"If you really think they're determined to destroy property," his dad continued, "you have other options. You could tell your coach your concern and let him handle it. You could make an anonymous, warning phone call to the other school. Or, if you really feel gutsy, you could stand up at tomorrow's pep rally and, as team co-captain, ask everyone to show good sportsmanship toward your archrival. You might be surprised at the reaction!"

The more Juan and his dad talked, the more options Juan discovered.

Important decisions are seldom easy. There are usually several options. This is a great opportunity for free-flowing discussion as kids sort through their values and priorities.

In Juan's situation, he also needs to look into the future and attach possible consequences to each potential decision. But Juan needs his dad's wisdom and experience to look into the future. As the two work together, Juan will become a more responsible decision-maker.

GET HELP

Our kids shouldn't make decisions alone—as though they were isolated on an island with no one to guide them. Kids can learn from the experiences and foibles of others. And they can learn from other people's knowledge and expertise. Gathering additional information can help them understand and balance their options.

As your teenager is shifting and shuffling options, he or she may need additional help. Encourage your teenager to do a little research. Suggest some of these sources:

● *A home resource library*—You don't need bookshelves or a squeaky, swiveling magazine rack. You don't need to create a sophisticated card-catalog system. All you need is to keep an eye open for resources that might help your teenager make decisions. The "Decision-Making Resources" box on page 58 suggests some information to include.

● *Prayer*—Asking for God's guidance and leadership in our decisions is central to making Christian decisions. It's important that we nurture our teenagers in this spiritual aspect of making good decisions.

Prayer is also a reminder that, no matter what decisions we make, God is always with us. He is indeed our refuge and strength through good times and bad.

● *Scripture*—The Bible is filled with good advice for different decisions your teenager will make. It's also filled with stories of people who made tough decisions. Encouraging your teenager to make scripture a central part of the decision-making process will help him or her apply faith to everyday life.

● *Experts*—Your teenager may need advice and a new perspective from someone other than a parent. Don't hesitate to refer your teenager to a pastor, lawyer, financial counselor, school principal or whoever can give useful guidance. An outside person may suggest options that never occurred to you.

EXAMINE YOUR FAITH

*A*t a youth camp one summer, some girls delighted in making fun of Gloria. She was extremely overweight, making it hard for her to walk the trails or participate in games.

Lisa felt sorry for Gloria and angry toward her friends who teased Gloria. She tried to say something to the leaders, but they didn't seem concerned. Never once did Lisa see an adult try to befriend Gloria.

Lisa couldn't decide what to do. If she befriended Gloria, she knew she'd be ridiculed. And she'd probably be Gloria's only friend for the whole week. If she confronted her friends, they'd probably shut her out. She'd still end up with Gloria.

That night, Lisa went to the camp director and explained her concern. "I don't know what to do," Lisa said, nearly in tears.

"You're a special person to care so much," the director told her. Then the director took out a Bible and turned to Matthew 5:7-9. "I use this passage a lot during camp. When you hear it, you'll know why."

Then the director read: "Happy are those who are merciful to others; God will be merciful to them! Happy are the pure in heart; they will see God! Happy are those who work for peace;

DECISION-MAKING RESOURCES

*H*ere are some key resources to keep in your home resource library to help your teenager hone decision-making skills:

• *Bible*—It's important to teach our teenagers that faith plays a central role in decision-making. The Bible is filled with great drama that comes out of good and bad decisions. It's filled with important values, advice and guidance. What kind of decision does God want me to make? It's a question that ought to be asked repeatedly.

• *Music, movies and television*—In many ways, the media reflect life's mysteries, joys, problems and desires. Songs can offer great opportunities for examining decisions. A TV show may explore an issue your teenager faces. A movie can open doors for discussions of choices and values.

Even songs, TV shows and movies with negative themes can be used to help your teenager think through choices. If you hear a song with a negative message, talk about how a Christian should respond responsibly. Do the same thing when you watch television or when your teenager goes to a movie.

• *Books or tapes*—Look for self-improvement books or tapes at your library or bookstore. Encourage your teenager to look for solid advice from Christian thinkers. Pick up books on topics that are on your teenager's mind.

One resource is the What Would *You* Do? series (Teenage Books, Box 481, Loveland, CO 80539). These Christian books are fast-reading fiction in which the

continued

readers' choices guide the outcome of the stories. The approach helps kids examine their options and see consequences. The books deal with topics such as sexuality, drugs, family life, sports and friendship.

● *Newspaper and magazine articles*—Clip articles about issues your teenager is dealing with, such as dating, college and part-time jobs. Then have the articles available as resources when your teenager is sorting through options.

The news is also filled with dramatic stories of people who make difficult decisions. Some are heart-warming. Others are tragic. Look for poignant stories, cut them out and underline key parts. Then stick them on your teenager's bulletin board. Lay them on his pillow. Tape them to her bedroom ceiling. Put it under the windshield wiper on his car. If you take time to be creative and fun, your teenager will take time to read the clipping.

● *Brochures and pamphlets*—Brochures and pamphlets are everywhere! Church. Library. Community college. Bank. Post Office. Doctor's office. Drugstore. And most are free! They deal with all kinds of personal, health and social issues. Pin a pamphlet to your teenager's bath towel. Tape it to a mirror. Hang it inside the refrigerator. Then ask about it later.

● *Games*—Certain board games demand that players make good decisions, considering the consequences and options. Chess strategy, for example, involves plotting your course, then being flexible, depending on your opponent's moves. Numerous available board games can be vehicles for teaching decision-making, including The Hunt for Red October; I Think, You Think, I Think; and Monopoly.

God will call them his children!"

Then Lisa and the director talked about how the passage applied to Lisa's decision. The director posed the question: What would Jesus do? By the time Lisa left that evening, she knew what she needed to do.

The next day at lunch, Lisa marched into the dining hall with Gloria. She went over to a table of her friends. "Everyone, I'd like you to meet Gloria," Lisa beamed. "This is her first year at camp, and she'd like to get to know all of you. I told her this is the best gang in the whole camp!"

Lisa and Gloria became good friends that day. And the others discovered Gloria's wonderful, off-the-wall sense of humor. Soon Gloria was the hit of the week.

Challenging our kids to include Christ in their decisions helps them exercise their faith. It also reminds them that Christians never have to make decisions alone.

EVALUATE THE DECISION

Once your teenager has made a decision, help him or her look back at the options to be sure it's the best choice. Encourage your teenager to give the decision time to soak in.

Here are some questions for your teenager to ask (or for you to ask your teenager) to help evaluate the choice:

- Is it a good decision? Is it a Christian decision?
- Does it get you where you want to be now? in the future?
- What are the immediate consequences of the decision?
- What are the long-range consequences?
- Can you live with the consequences?

● Will your decision and consequences hurt anyone?

● Now, should you reconsider your decision?

Marsha, 15, had had it! Before the summer, she thought she'd enjoy working with kids in the city's parks program. But the experience was awful. She couldn't control the kids; some were only three years younger than her. And her partner ...

Well, her partner was older but not much help. She spent the afternoons sunbathing instead of leading recreation activities. So Marsha was stuck with all the work.

Toward the end of the summer, the parks director asked Marsha if she'd reapply for the next year. No way, she thought! This stuff wasn't for her. But she decided not to say anything right away. She'd think about it a little longer.

The next morning, Marsha went to the director to say how hard the summer had been. "I wish you'd told me earlier," the director said. "I think you have real gifts working with children. I would've done something about your partner. Please reconsider."

"I'm not sure," Marsha responded. "But I'll think about it."

That night, after talking with her mom, Marsha realized the director might be right. So she applied for the next summer.

And the next. And the next. And the next. And the next.

Marsha ended up spending six summers working with kids and using her creative gifts to learn puppetry, games and other leadership skills. She might've never discovered those skills if it hadn't been for an encouraging director and Marsha's willingness to re-evaluate her decision.

DECISION-MAKING DISCUSSIONS

A creative way to help teenagers explore decision-making is to spend time together exercising their (and your) decision-making skills. Here's a format to follow:

● ***Review your family's day.*** Start by talking about decisions each person made during the day or week.

● ***Introduce a situation.*** Present a decision-making dilemma. Your situation ideas may come from anywhere. News stories. Personal dilemmas. Or use the scenarios on page 63.

● ***Discuss options.*** Use the guidelines described in this chapter. Don't dismiss any option. You'll have opportunities to evaluate options later.

● ***Role play consequences.*** Have each family member take a role in a situation, then respond to the situation from that person's perspective. This process can open up other options and help you evaluate each one.

● ***Discuss more, then decide.*** Begin evaluating the options. Consult the Bible and other resources for guidance. Keep charts of pros and cons. Then decide.

● ***Close with prayer.*** Ask God to guide you in the real-life decisions each family member makes every day.

PRACTICE DECISION-MAKING

*E*ffectively using the decision-making process described in this chapter takes practice. Exploring hypothetical situations helps our teenagers when they're faced with real-life choices. This chapter concludes with 12 scenarios you can use with your teenager to practice.

The scenarios reflect various dilemmas. Some are taken from scripture. Others deal with contemporary problems. Others are just plain fun. Use them whenever you have time to talk. Or pull them out when you use the format described in the "Decision-Making Discussions" box on page 62.

Expand on the scenarios. Change them. Turn them into tools that sharpen your teenager's skills.

● *Scenario #1*—As you're arriving for a youth group meeting, you see two group members drinking beer in their car before going into the church. What do you do?

● *Scenario #2*—You're going to your uncle's funeral. He was a professional clown. Your cousins are going in clown outfits to honor his memory. They want you to do the same. Your parents don't know anything about this scheme. What do you do?

● *Scenario #3*—You see your Sunday school teacher shoplifting. What do you do?
Variations:
● The shoplifter is the minister's wife.
● The shoplifter is the minister's son and your good friend.
● The shoplifter is an elderly church member.
● The shoplifter is your best friend's sister.

● *Scenario #4*—You're simple fishermen who have families to support. Jesus asks you to give up what you're doing and follow him. You're barely making a living as it is, but his manner is enthralling. What do you do?

● *Scenario #5*—You've been on a date with someone you really like. On the way home, you stop in the park to talk. The passion begins heating up. What do you do?

Variations:

● It's your first date with this person.

● You've been going out together for a year.

● You've been going steady for a year, and your date is leaving for college the next day. You won't see each other for three months.

● *Scenario #6*—An admiring person of the opposite sex calls you and invites you over for the evening. The parents are gone for the weekend, so you can stay as late as you want. What do you do?

Variations:

● Your parents are also gone for the weekend.

● The person inviting you has a bad reputation.

● The person inviting you is your best friend's "steady."

● The person says he or she wants to study with you.

● *Scenario #7*—Your boss, who you dislike intensely, is about to make a speech to the employees. You notice his **pants** are unzipped. What do you do?

● *Scenario #8*—You get a D on your report card. You're sure your parents will ground you for the rest of your life! A friend advises you to change the grade—from a D to a B—by using just a little creative writing. Your parents will never know, your friend assures you. What do you do?

● *Scenario #9*—Someone offers crack cocaine to you and your friends—for free. Your friends take some. It's your turn. What do you do?

● *Scenario #10*—You're babysitting for neighbors. They've rented a video for you to enjoy while they're gone. When you play it, you discover that the video store must've accidentally given them an X-rated movie. You're all alone, and the kids are in bed. What do you do?
Variations:
● You're babysitting your pastor's kids.
● As you're looking through their video drawer, you discover several other X-rated movies.
● Your friends stop over, see the video and beg you to play the whole thing.

● *Scenario #11*—You are Peter, Jesus' disciple. Jesus has been arrested. Someone sees you and accuses you of being one of Jesus' cronies. The authorities grab you and ask you to confess. Your confession will almost certainly be your death sentence. What do you do?

● *Scenario #12*—There's a new person in your class with a different ethnic background. Most of your classmates ignore her—even make fun of her. At lunch you see her sitting alone at a table. The kids you're with make a point of sitting at the opposite end of the cafeteria. What do you do?

CHAPTER**FIVE**

❖

DECISION-MAKING POWER TOOLS

❖

Have you ever tried to cut a sheet of half-inch plywood with a crosscut saw? If you're like me, it's not a pretty sight. First, it takes forever, and your arm aches before you're halfway across. Then, once you've cut all the way through, you look at the edge. Chances are, it's ragged.

But give me an electric circular saw, and I do a fair job. I cut the board quickly, and the edge is relatively straight.

When it comes to decision-making, some people may have enough practice and a natural knack that they make good choices without much help. But the rest of us can save lots of time, effort and frustration if we use decision-making "power tools." Like the carpenter's circular saw, table saw and drill press, these power tools help shape responsible choices. This chapter is an "operators manual" for several of these tools.

ASKING GOOD QUESTIONS

*T*he first power tool for helping kids learn decision-making is to ask good questions. Asking our teenagers good questions gives them a compass they can use to determine their own direction and make their own discoveries. And when kids make their own discoveries, they don't forget them.

Sometimes it's hard to ask questions when we'd rather give answers. But I believe good, probing questions have five positive effects that make them worth the effort:

1. Good questions challenge teenagers to think. Why do you want to do that? Why do you feel that way? What's bothering you? When asked with respect, these questions help teenagers look inward and examine the causes and effects of their actions.

2. Good questions put responsibility where it belongs. What do you think you should do now? How are you going to respond? Good questions imply that we may not have the answers. Maybe our teenagers have the answers to their problems and don't know it.

3. Good questions enlighten. Think about it. What kind of teacher inspires you more: one who constantly makes statements of fact? Or one who always asks questions? (There, feel enlightened?)

4. Good questions teach critical thinking. Questions that require more than yes-or-no answers prevent our teenagers from jumping to quick conclusions. Good questions force kids to think through their answers before responding.

5. Good questions open kids' minds to other perspectives and options. "Have you ever thought about ... ?" can open a door that our kids may not have known even existed.

With the value of questions in mind, let's look at some questions you can ask your teenager to hone decision-making skills:

● *May I help you? What's bothering you?* These are simple, non-combative questions. They're polite ways of entering your teenager's world where you may discover a festering, unresolved decision. They're positive prods that don't pry.

Mike looked distracted at the dinner table one night. When his dad asked what was bothering him, Mike just shrugged. He sat there and continued to pick at his food.

After some insistence from his dad, Mike opened up and shared what was bothering him. The boy whose locker was next to his asked Mike to hide some Playboy magazines in his locker. He told Mike someone else knew the combination to his own locker and was trying to steal the magazines. Mike agreed to stash them in his locker.

After the next period was over, Mike went to his locker and swung the door open. The magazines fell out all over the hallway, in full view of everyone. A teacher walked by, saw the magazines, and collared Mike.

Since this happened near the end of the school day, the teacher told Mike to see him first thing in the morning. They'd go have a chat with the principal.

Mike had spent the rest of the afternoon thinking about what would happen tomorrow morning. It took some prodding, but his dad was able to help Mike once Mike began opening up.

● *What are your options?* Chapter four explored the importance of looking at all the options. Presenting those options in the form of questions lets our teenagers discover the possibilities. If we dictate the options, our kids are unlikely to choose any of the options we present. And we also risk leaving out important possibilities.

THE LECTURE TRAP

We've been there before. We know what'll happen if our kids do what they've chosen. It'll be a disaster, we're sure. Our first reaction is to lecture—to pound our point home, hoping to influence our kids to change their minds. Why waste time with questions when the outcome is clear?

But we need to remember that lectures shut down the thinking process. If we constantly fill in the blanks with our own answers, why should our kids bother to think. They have little to do but follow orders.

What should you do when you feel a lecture coming on?

● Put yourself in your teenager's shoes. Do you like being lectured at? Then ask yourself: Even though I know it's a bad decision, why does my teenager think it's right?

● Think about your point, then ask questions to raise the issue.

● Only ask questions. Try not to speak in statements.

● Before you utter a word, take time to write some good questions and organize your thoughts.

● Consider this question: "Could I be wrong?"

Deanne's mom was sure her daughter should go to her own alma mater for college. "It's such a great school!" she'd exclaim over and over. "You'll love it there."

"But what would I study there?" Deanne would ask.

"Oh, just about anything," her mom would say enthusiastically. "English, physics, business, computer science—just about anything you want."

What her mom was forgetting was that Deanne had a special talent for music. And her mom's alma mater didn't have a music school. By pressuring her daughter, Deanne's mom may be cutting off an important option for her daughter.

● *What's your plan?* Dan, a young man in my youth group, used to tell me things he wouldn't think of discussing with his parents. Sometimes I think Dan told me things for shock value. He mainly just wanted a reaction—either positive or negative.

One day he walked into my office and announced he'd started dating one of the girls in the group. With a glint in his eye, he boasted that they'd almost "gone the whole way" the previous weekend. He implied sexual intercourse was inevitable before long.

I tried not to react. "What's your plan?" I asked him plainly.

"What do you mean?" he shot back.

"If you do go all the way and she gets pregnant," I continued, "what's your plan?"

Dan laughed. "She's not going to get pregnant. D'you think we're stupid? We have protection."

"No," I replied. "That's why I figure you have it all thought out. No birth control is 100 percent safe, so there's the chance she'll get pregnant. Because there's a chance, you should have a plan."

Dan tried to shrug it off. I could tell my question had caught him off-guard. No anger. No judgment. Just "what's your plan?" His coolness was cooling off.

I decided to keep firing. "Let's just suppose she does get pregnant. Will you tell her to get an abortion? Will you dump her and the child? Will you get a job and give up sports? Will you get married right away? Where will you live? What about college—for either of you? Will your parents support you? Will they help you through the financial crunch? Will hers?"

I looked him straight in the eye. "What's your plan, Dan?"

I don't think Dan ever followed through with his personal conquest. I don't think he'd thought about anything beyond a few moments of sexual excitement. When he was forced to think beyond his sex drive, it all became incredibly unromantic, practical and real.

The question, "What's your plan?" sets responsibility squarely on teenagers' shoulders. And finding answers forces teenagers to organize their thinking and to examine their future seriously.

● *Can you live with your choice?* Teenagers often make decisions based on what's good for today, tomorrow or, at best, next week. As parents, we need to remind them to look beyond today to see possible long-term consequences.

Nancy desperately wanted her own car. And she wanted it to be a red Honda Accord. She diligently saved $1,000 by working part time, then started looking. Her plan was to not spend more than $1,000, but she soon realized she wouldn't find what she wanted for that price.

But she did find one for $2,500. "It's a great deal," she told her dad. "It's still in good shape, and these cars don't need much maintenance. I *really* like it." Then she sprung the question:

"Can you loan me the extra money? I'll pay it all back."

Nancy's dad knew it had taken a year to earn the $1,000. And Nancy had said she'd start saving for college now. So he asked, "Have you calculated how long it would take to pay it all back?"

"It won't be long," she insisted. "I'll cut back on shopping and fun stuff. I can work more hours too."

So her dad kept asking questions. "What'll happen to your schoolwork if you work more hours? Do you really want to give up all your social life during your senior year? How are you going to pay for insurance and gas and repairs, if there are any? Is getting this exact car worth what you'll have to pay?"

Slowly, Nancy realized how miserable she'd be if she spent more than she'd saved to buy that car. She rethought her goal, and decided she'd have just as much fun and independence in a used Chevy that needed a paint job. By probing whether Nancy could live with her choice, her dad helped her make a responsible decision.

INSTILLING HOPE

*D*espite what we sometimes think, most kids worry about the world and the future. A Gallup Youth Survey found that the top five concerns of teenagers are drug abuse, alcohol abuse, teenage pregnancy, peer pressure and AIDS. And another survey by the University of Michigan found that 30 percent of high school seniors worry "a great deal" or "quite often" about social problems in the nation or world. Another 50 percent worry "sometimes."

At the same time, most teenagers don't see things improving much. For example, 41 percent of teenagers think poverty will get worse; 47 percent believe unemployment will increase; and 51 percent say crime will become a bigger problem.

As kids look at the future, why should they bother to care? If life is a dead end, there's little purpose in concerning oneself with directions and choices. What's the point of trying to make intelligent decisions if there's really not much worth living for? Perhaps they should just say, with the writer of Ecclesiastes, "It is useless, useless ... Life is useless, all useless" (Ecclesiastes 1:2).

Or perhaps the problem is that we adults aren't presenting the positive side of life to our kids. We're not giving them confidence that they *can* make a difference.

When teachers quizzed Jenny about her sliding grades and negative attitude, she tearfully told about her home life. "My parents hate everything," she said. "My dad says the world is a cesspool. It's full of crooks. Corporations are run by swindlers. The government doesn't care about anybody. And he hates his job because they're all jerks. He complains about everything. I don't think he even likes *me*. And my mom says her life is boring."

No wonder Jenny was distraught! Adding to her negativism, she explained how her parents were always harping at her to get straight A's. "If you ever want to amount to anything," her dad would yell, "you'd better be on the honor roll. There's college, which isn't cheap!"

Jenny was totally confused. Her mom had been an honor student and now her life was dull and meaningless. "Why try?" Jenny argued. "What's the use of working hard and getting good grades so I can work in a boring trap?"

Because of their own experiences, Jenny's parents were killing their daughter's spirit and drowning her hopes with their doomsday attitude.

We need to be reminded that most of what is wrong in our world is attributable to people! And most of what appears to be hopeless can be turned around. That's our responsibility too.

Rather than retreat from problems, we need to tackle life with renewed hope. We need to give ourselves and our kids a "faith-lift." We need to help our kids see that their decisions will count for something.

If you have trouble finding hope, try these "hope helps":

● *Find and share examples of ordinary people making extraordinary differences in your community and the world.* Read your local newspaper. Let your teenager see that ordinary people live lives full of hope and promise.

● *Get involved in hope-making activities.* Work together as a family to make a difference in your community. Help build homes for Habitat for Humanity to give low-income families new hope for the future. Recycle at home to show your concern for the future. Plant an oak tree as a gift for the future.

● *Discuss ways the world is a better, safer and healthier place than it used to be.* Talk to grandparents or other senior citizens about the hard and scary times they've faced. Watch for new scientific and medical breakthroughs that overcome problems of the past. Celebrate progress when you see it.

● *Discuss stories of people who succeeded in spite of the naysayers around them.* Talk about people who refused to give up hope. For example, someone once told Walt Disney he had no artistic talent! A music teacher told his student he'd never compose anything worthwhile. That student was Ludwig von Beethoven.

● *Rely on God for the future.* Our faith offers us hope for the future and for life after death. It's this hope that remains strong 2,000 years after Jesus' Resurrection.

DISCIPLINING WITH CHOICES

*T*here's no better way to teach our teenagers responsibility than to offer them choices when we discipline. It's hard to do. It takes skill and patience. But if we learn to replace our parental pride with humility, we can teach our kids how to weigh tough choices by giving them tough choices.

Mary violated her curfew one too many times. Her parents reasoned with her and threatened her. Nothing worked. Finally, they let her decide her punishment. She could . . .

1. give up going out with friends for three weekends;

2. make her curfew one hour earlier on weekends; or

3. call home every hour whenever she's out to tell her parents where she is and when she's coming home.

For Mary, the first option was out of the question. No way would she stay home three weekends! The second one would really cramp her style. Just when things would really start hopping on Saturday night, she'd have to go home. Talk about humiliating! The third choice would make her feel like a baby.

All three seemed impossible to live with, Mary concluded. But she had to choose one. She'll have to do some hard thinking. And you can be sure Mary will consider the consequences carefully before she breaks curfew again.

To be effective, discipline choices should . . .

● *Relate to the misconduct.* If the choices are too far removed from the negative behavior, they lose their positive impact. That's why Mary's options all relate to curfews. The connections between the problem and the consequence are clear.

● *Remind teenagers of the misconduct.* While teenagers mull over their discipline choices, they'll also play back the negative behavior repeatedly. And they'll be more apt to think before acting next time.

● *Force teenagers to weigh options carefully.* The process of choosing a punishment helps teenagers think about their behavior and the resulting discipline. In Mary's case, she had to choose between three options she didn't like. Comparing the options helps teenagers make decisions in the future.

● *Be fair but firm.* The choices need to be reasonable. But they also need to require sacrifice. Otherwise, the decisions won't be difficult or the consequences thought-provoking.

CLARIFYING EXPECTATIONS

When the issue of curfew came up in my home, my parents spelled it out clearly. "We trust you to make the right decision," they assured me. "First, here's what we expect: You'll go to school and church. And you'll do your best to get good grades. Other than that, you do what you think is best. We won't give you a curfew; we think you can set a reasonable time for yourself.

*"You said I could decorate my
room just like I wanted."*

Just let us know where you are so we won't worry about you."

It was as simple as that. As long as I met their specific expectations, I could enjoy the privilege of deciding what to do with the rest of my busy life. I was free ... within a framework.

Kids want freedom. But they also want and need the structure of our expectations. Our expectations can be the foundation upon which our kids will build their decision-making skills.

"Do whatever you want" is permission not to choose.

"Decide for yourself as long as you understand what I expect" gives teenagers a sense of responsibility and independence.

Our expectations should be:

● *Clear*—Kids won't have any idea of what we expect unless we explain those expectations clearly.

"Well, uh ... I really wish you could help me sometime so I can get the house painted ... " This kind of fuzzy request leaves things wide open for interpretation—and misunderstanding.

"I want you to help me paint the house next Saturday." This approach leaves no doubt.

● *Reasonable and fair*—Expectations shouldn't be unreasonably strict or unrealistic. "I want you to spend four hours every day doing homework and one hour practicing tuba" is certainly clear, but it probably isn't realistic in most teenagers' busy, erratic schedules. Remember, we're asking our kids to live up to our expectations, not to collapse under them.

● *Firm*—If our expectations are too flexible, they won't represent consistent standards. Unless we uphold our expectations and the consequences, our kids will think we don't really expect what we say we expect. And thus we'll give no guidance.

TOUGH TEACHING CHOICES

*H*ere are some teenage "misdemeanors" and effective choices to teach responsible (and tough) decision-making. Which would you choose if you were in each teenager's shoes? Which do you think your teenager would choose? Talk about the choices together as a family.

1. The police stop John for reckless driving, then leave it to his parents to discipline their son. John's parents give him three choices:

(a) Write an apology to the community for his careless driving and submit it to the newspaper. He'd also walk everywhere he needed to go for two weeks.

(b) Visit car-accident victims in the hospital every other day after school for a month.

(c) Forfeit his driver's license for one month.

2. Phyllis' teacher informs her parents that Phyllis constantly disrupts class with talking and laughing. With the teacher's cooperation, the parents give Phyllis three options:

(a) Agree that her parents would call the teacher every day for three weeks for a report on Phyllis' behavior.

(b) Write a contract promising not to be disruptive. Then read it to the class.

(c) Take an "incomplete" in the class and sit in the principal's office during that period.

● *High but reachable*—Our expectations should challenge our kids to stretch. But they shouldn't be so high that they guarantee failure. Constant failure leads to despair.

PRAYING ABOUT DECISIONS

A mother of three teenagers told me her family joins hands around the dinner table each evening and asks God to help each family member make the right choices. The oldest boy thinks it's corny, she confesses. But he does it anyway. And when she forgets, the kids remind her. For her family, prayer has become a family practice—and a valuable decision-making tool.

One comment she made really stuck with me. "You know, when I pray out loud and ask God to help us make the right decision about something, I think it's good for my kids. They see that I don't just make family decisions because I think I'm so smart. I think they appreciate that I ask for help too. They realize that ol' Mom doesn't have all the answers."

"We get real specific in our prayers," she told me. "When we're faced with a real tough one, we say: 'Okay, Lord, we have a, b, or c. Help us decide which is best.' "

A typical prayer at the family's dinner table might be: "Dear God, please help Tom make the right decision about his car. Should he sell it? or try to fix it? Lord, we've talked a lot about it. We need your guidance."

In Matthew 26:36-39, Jesus went to the Garden of Gethsemane to pray in the face of his agonizing decision. "My Father," he prayed, "if it is possible, take this cup of suffering from me! Yet not what I want, but what you want." Jesus asked God to help him make the right decision.

If prayer isn't already part of your family's decision-making process, use these do's and don'ts to help you integrate prayer into your decisions:

● *DO make prayer a regular family practice.* Prayer shouldn't be used like a fire extinguisher—only in an emergency. Pray together every day and ask God for ongoing guidance in the decisions you make.

● *DON'T forget to pray.* Often we get so busy trying to make things right ourselves that we forget to pray. Prayer should be our first and ongoing response when making an important decision.

● *DO listen for an answer.* Take some time to listen for a response to your prayer. Sometimes there's an obvious one, but we're too busy to notice it.

● *DON'T pray to put on a show.* Your vocabulary and style are inconsequential in God's eyes. Teach your teenager the privacy of prayer (Matthew 6:6).

● *DO include the question: "Lord, what would you have us do?"* Sometimes we wait for God to do something miraculous to tell us exactly what to do. This question puts the decision back in our hands to act on God's leading.

PLUGGING 'EM IN AND GOING TO WORK

I 'm not a mechanical genius. But thanks to my dad, I have at least a survivalist's knowledge of how to use tools. When I was quite young, my dad let me tighten the vise or operate the drill press. And he'd patiently show me how to use the other tools in his extensive workshop.

I'll never tear down and rebuild an engine. But I do know enough to cover everyday headaches. And that gets me by okay. I'm glad Dad had the knowledge and patience to teach me.

The suggestions in this chapter are a lot like the power tools in my dad's workshop. None of them do much good if they sit on the shelf. And none can be mastered without practice.

But the more you use them and teach your teenager how to use them, the more skilled you'll become at guiding your teenager's decisions. And the more your teenager will develop the skills needed to make responsible choices.

CHAPTER**SIX**

❖

10 VOWS OF CARING PARENTS

❖

Teenagers are pretty confident of their invincibility. They'll try things just because they haven't tried them before. They'll do dumb things on a dare just to be accepted by peers. They'll be totally irresponsible when we're sure they know better.

Sometimes the mistakes are relatively insignificant: minor car mishaps; stupid pranks; flunking tests. And we can laugh about them later in life.

But other mistakes can be tragic: drinking and driving; premarital sex; drug use; dropping out of school. They change the future.

We parents become frustrated, trying to keep our kids from making poor choices. But no matter how much teaching, coaxing, protecting, pleading and screaming we do, we'll occasionally clean up after incredibly thoughtless, irresponsible decisions made by our teenagers.

So we need to take the "10 Vows of a Caring Parent." We need to review them often and put them into practice. They'll help us—and our kids—grow through the tough times.

1. I'LL BE THERE FOR YOU

"*A* few weeks ago my father caught me in a lie," a high school sophomore told me recently. "It wasn't that big a deal, but he thought it was a really big deal."

The teenager shrugged, then continued. "We talked about it for a long time. Dad told me that no matter what I did or how bad it was, he'd always be there for me. I gained a great deal of respect for him. And now, even when I mess up, I know I don't have to lie about it."

Being there for our kids, no matter what the cost, brings greater understanding and respect between us and our teenagers. It tells our kids they can count on us; they need not go elsewhere when things go wrong.

2. I'LL LOVE YOU NO MATTER WHAT

A dad made an unsettling observation about the consistency and quality of our love for our kids. You can bet, he said, that if we don't shower our kids with love and affection—especially when they screw up horribly—they'll turn to someone who will offer what appears to be love. That someone may be a criminal, a psycho, a cult leader or a smart profiteer.

When Yolanda sneaked out of the house in the middle of the night, she didn't think her mom would ever find out. But her mom did.

"We had a long talk about how much she trusted me before I made this stupid mistake," Yolanda recalls. "She said I made her trust in me go down."

Yolanda got grounded for a month. But, she says, she appreciated her mom's response. "Mom told me how much she loved me. We agreed I never should've done it. And I said I'd never do it again."

As parents, we can learn about unconditional love from our heavenly father. As Romans 8:38-39 states: "For I am certain that ... there is nothing in all creation that will ever be able to separate us from the love of God which is ours through Christ Jesus our Lord."

3. I'LL LOVE YOU "TOUGHLY"

*L*oving our kids doesn't mean ignoring their bad decisions. Excusing a poor decision doesn't show love and affection. It shows a lack of caring.

To love "toughly" means to love while teaching accountability. One parent said it this way: "When kids make bad decisions, parents shouldn't try to soften the disappointment by giving them consolation prizes."

Kids need to feel the pain of a bad decision—their own pain and the pain they may have caused others. It doesn't hurt to hurt once in a while.

I'll never forget Adam. He and his parents were active church members and solid citizens. One weekend Adam's parents went out of town. Adam and his best friend decided to sneak Adam's parents' sports car out for a Saturday-night spin. They bought a six-pack of beer and headed out to a popular country road where kids "tested" their cars.

Several beers later, the two boys were zooming around the curves. Suddenly, the car careened out of control and hit a telephone pole. Adam was thrown clear. But his best friend was killed instantly.

For weeks, Adam awoke screaming in the middle of the night. He saw the accident over and over in his mind. He heard the crunch of metal. He tasted blood. He saw the mangled body of his best friend.

Adam wondered why his best friend was dead, instead of him. His parents were advised to keep a close watch on him for fear he might try to even the score by killing himself.

In spite of the anguish, Adam's parents insisted that he live with the legal consequences of his actions. They didn't try to make excuses for him or get him a reduced sentence because of "mental anguish." They didn't want his friend's death to excuse their son from experiencing the full impact of his actions.

Adam lost his driver's license for two years, and he was heavily fined. He was also ordered to perform 500 hours of community service in a hospital, working with injured victims of alcohol-related accidents.

Tough, tough love. But Adam's parents never abandoned him. They forced him to confront the consequences of his tragic decision, but they loved him every step of the way.

4. I'LL LOVE YOU IN THE REAL WORLD

"If I had it to do over again," one parent said, "I'd let my kids experience a few more of the harsh realities of life. I've never let them see people's negativism."

Because of a birth defect, Cheryl walked with a limp. But she didn't let that stop her. She was a member in school clubs, captain of the girls volleyball team, and the best cheerleader on the varsity squad. Everyone liked Cheryl.

So Cheryl was devastated when her dad was transferred and the family had to move to a new town. Suddenly Cheryl was a stranger. She was the new girl in school who walked funny. Making friends was tough.

But Cheryl was determined. She decided to try out for cheerleading. Her parents warned her that her handicap might keep her from being selected since no one knew her well enough to look beyond her limp. But they didn't override her decision.

Cheryl didn't even make the finals. Though she was deeply disappointed, her parents had prepared her by giving her an honest glimpse of the real world. Her parents assured her that next time her chances would be better.

Disappointing decisions aren't necessarily bad decisions. They may just be ill-timed or misplaced. Similarly, a good decision can wind up in disaster simply because life isn't always fair. Our kids need to learn that.

5. I'LL HELP YOU LEARN FROM FAILURE

*P*eople seldom talk about all of Thomas Edison's flops. Or Babe Ruth's record-setting strikeouts. Or George Washington's surrender during the French and Indian War. Most great people have failed many times—either because they made poor choices or something didn't work out as they'd anticipated. But they became great because they were willing to take risks and, as a consequence, make mistakes.

This poem illustrates the point:

> A mistake
> > is
> > > a stepping stone.
>
> If I am not
> allowed a mistake,
> I will not
> step.

Think of God's relationship with us. He gives us the free will to fall on our faces. But he always loves us and is always there to pick us up, if we let him. Our kids need to discover that our love for them and God's love for them is unceasing, even when they really blow it!

6. I'LL HELP YOU REALIZE THAT AN UNCERTAIN DECISION IS BETTER THAN NO DECISION

*D*uring her junior year, Melanie was invited to study theater in England during the summer. It was a dream come true. But Steve, her boyfriend, pleaded with her to stay home and work with him in his father's hardware store.

Months passed. Melanie wrote letters to England requesting more time to think about her decision. She also put off Steve until she could find out if the school would grant her an extension in accepting the invitation. But Steve was growing more and more impatient.

Finally, Steve's father hired someone else to work in the store. And Steve, in a fit of anger, told Melanie to get lost. Soon after, she received a notice from England that the overseas study offer was no longer available to her. Someone else had been invited.

That summer, Melanie watched as her friends landed good summer jobs. It was too late for her to apply—all the jobs were filled. There she was at home—dejected—with no options whatsoever.

There's nothing wrong with deciding not to decide right away. That's still a decision. The problem comes when we never commit to anything for fear of being wrong. Nothing gets done because we won't make a crucial decision.

Only by making critical decisions will our teenagers truly learn and grow and get somewhere. The alternative is to stand at

"But what happens if I take the wrong exit?"

the fork in the road, forever looking in both directions as others pass them by.

7. I WON'T PUNISH YOU FOR MAKING A DIFFERENT DECISION THAN I'D MAKE

"*P*lease let your kids make some of their own decisions," a ninth-grader urged parents. "And if a decision isn't what you hoped it would be, stand by your kids. Love them still. Don't punish them for making a decision you wouldn't make."

Will's parents were furious when he came home from a party at 2:30 a.m.—2 1/2 hours after his midnight curfew. The 17-year-old tried to explain that some of the guys needed rides home, and he'd volunteered to take them.

"Why didn't you tell them to walk?" his dad said angrily. "You knew when you were supposed to be home."

"We were worried sick," Will's mother joined in.

Will didn't want to tell them everything, but finally he had to. "Some of the guys had a few drinks, and some of the rest of us didn't want to let them drive," he explained reluctantly. "I drove the drinkers, and others followed in their cars."

Will paused. "I knew I'd be late, but I thought it was important."

Will's dad wasn't so sure. "Why didn't you let those jerks find their own way home? They didn't deserve taxi service!"

"I wasn't concerned only about them, Dad," Will said. "I was worried about some of the people who'd be riding with those jerks. Some of us felt it was better to get them home. Then no one would get hurt.'

Will's mother finally agreed that he'd made a smart decision. But his dad stubbornly reminded him that "I would've taken their car keys away from them and let the bums crawl home!"

Will was upset and confused by his father's anger. He'd made what he thought was a responsible choice—one that might've saved lives. Yet his father couldn't accept his son's decision, simply because he would've done it differently. It took several conversations to finally convince him that Will had made a good choice to keep the "bums" off the road.

Throughout this book, I've suggested that there's more than one way to make a responsible choice. As parents, we need to accept—even celebrate—when our kids make responsible choices that aren't exactly what we would've done. It shows they're learning to be independently responsible.

8. I'LL TEACH YOU NOT TO BE ASHAMED TO SAY "I'M SORRY"

When Adam's reckless driving killed his best friend, his parents made him apologize to the bereaved family.

When a former student of mine started a fight at an "away" basketball game, he had to say "I'm sorry" to the entire student body—ours and theirs.

When friends of mine grounded their teenage daughter for two months, they later retracted their punishment with an apology when they realized they hadn't clearly communicated their expectations.

Saying "I'm sorry" is tough. But if we can say it when we ought to, our kids will say it more easily too. The consequences of a tragic decision can never be undone. But real maturity shines through when people can squarely face their responsibilities and apologize for bad decisions.

9. I'LL TRUST YOU WITH ANOTHER CHANCE

*H*uman beings make mistakes. Teenagers, too! When they do, it's important that we parents give them another chance.

I sometimes think of Jesus and his disciples as a kind of single-parent family. Jesus loved them no matter how many times they let him down. When they "screwed up," he never abandoned them. He didn't try to shield them from the harsh realities of the world, nor did he always bail them out of bad decisions. He taught them to think on their own, then commissioned them to go out and teach others. And in spite of their weaknesses and indecisiveness, Jesus gave them greater responsibilities as they grew and matured in their understanding.

Our teenagers, like the disciples, are flawed human beings. They'll disappoint us, betray our trust and break our hearts. But we should never stop loving them and trying to teach them. They deserve as many chances to get it right as God grants us.

And that's a limitless number!

10. I'LL ENCOURAGE YOU TO THINK FOR YOURSELF

When Brett was a sophomore, he told his parents he wanted to quit basketball and concentrate on photography and writing. Even though he played basketball well, his folks reluctantly agreed. "After all," Brett's mother commented, "we'd always taught Brett to think for himself."

As a senior, Brett's photo portfolio won the regional competition. He also won first place in the nation and a $1,000 scholarship in a short-story contest.

"It was his decision," his father said. "He owned it, and it was the right one. We were really proud of him."

Brett's parents had discovered the excitement that comes when we give our kids the freedom and skills to make their own responsible choices. As they learn to think for themselves, we'll be surprised—and delighted—at the wise, responsible choices they make that we never would've thought of ourselves.

● ● ●

When Gary told his mom he wanted to go live with his father in another city, she was stunned and hurt. "Gary, please talk with me about this," she pleaded. "You know legally I can make you stay."

Gary slouched down in his chair. "But why would you want to, Mom. If you know I don't like it here, why make me stay?"

His mother looked at him through moist eyes. "I don't understand, Gary. I thought we were doing okay. What's wrong all of the sudden?"

Gary sat silently, then cleared his throat softly. "Mom ... I always feel like you're smothering me—trying to protect me too much." There was a tense pause while Gary looked down at the faded linoleum floor. "Dad would let me do more," he said finally.

Gary's mother brought her hand down hard on the table. "If I seem overprotective, Gary, it's because you're all I've got!" She tried to calm herself. "If I didn't care about you, I'd let you do anything you wanted. Is that what you want?"

Gary sighed heavily. "I'm almost 17, Mom. I'm not sure I want to go to college. I want to travel—maybe work my way across the country or something. Or go live with Dad for a while."

"Or something," his mother returned sarcastically. She stood up. "If that's the way you want to live, then go. I won't try to stop you."

Gary looked up slowly. "Mom, I still love you."

"Yeah," she murmured. "Yeah, sure. Me too."

Gary's mother went to work early the next morning. She wasn't home to see Gary catch the taxi to the bus station.

Two months later, Gary's mom was fumbling for the house keys with groceries in her arms, when the door opened by itself. "Hi, Mom, you need some help?" a cheerful voice said.

Was it really her son smiling at her? She dropped her bags of groceries on the porch and threw her arms around him. "You scared me to death, you big jerk!" she said, laughing and crying. "Where did you come from?"

Gary pulled back but kept hold of her hands. "It's a long

story, Mom. I honestly don't know where I've been."

His mother looked puzzled. "You weren't with your father?"

Gary nodded. "Sort of," he said hesitantly. "But I'm back, Mom. Back to stay. That is, if I can come back."

His eyes dropped to the floor. "I know I hurt you. I'm sorry."

"What made you decide to come home?" she wanted to know. "When I didn't get any letters, I figured you were too busy doing everything you always wanted to do."

"I was there for two months, and I saw Dad maybe for a week. He was never home. And when he was, we didn't get along."

Gary smiled. "You were right, Mom. I was stupid for going." He paused. "Anyway," Gary said more brightly, "is my bedroom still available?"

His mother hugged him again. "Welcome home, honey." Then she looked at him sternly. "Next time you think I'm being a mother hen, let's talk about it." Her tone became gentle again. "I never stopped loving you, son."

"I know, Mom," he said quickly. "Same here. Thanks."

As our kids begin making their own choices, we'll sometimes feel frustrated, angry and rejected. Why does she do such stupid things? Why doesn't he ever learn? What did I do wrong?

But in the midst of the struggles, we watch our kids grow in their understanding and learn from their mistakes. We see them making mature, responsible choices. And we marvel at their abilities to make tough decisions we never faced.

And then, someday, when our kids will come to us and say, "Thanks," we'll know the energy we used in helping our teenagers learn responsibility was well spent.